WHEN

GOD'S

PEOPLE

PRAY

DR. SAM OWUSU

ISBN 978-1-926652-41-2

Published by DaySprings Publishing, Surrey, BC. Canada.

For information, contact the publisher at

info@dayspringspublishing.com

Or contact the author at info@calvaryonline.ca

CONTENTS

CONTENTS

ACKNOWLEDGEMENTS

A work of this kind is not completed without the
collaboration of many people.
I wish to thank the following people for
their important contribution to this book.

Thank you Maughan Mariani, for your long hours of
transcribing and editing my sermons.

Thank you my faithful friend Henry Agbozo, for your
encouragement to write this book and helping me to
publish it.

I also thank my wife, Rosemond, for allowing me to get
away to hibernate to write this book. Thank you for your
understanding and support, asking me daily how the
book was progressing and praying for me during this
process.

And above all, thanks be to God for His anointing and
unspeakable grace.

THIS BOOK IS DEDICATED TO ALL THE MEMBERS OF
CALVARY WORSHIP CENTER .

THANK YOU FOR YOUR FAITHFULNESS AND
SUPPORT IN MAKING OUR CHURCH
TO BE TRULY A CHURCH OF PRAYER FOR
ALL NATIONS.

YOU TRULY KNOW WHAT HAPPENS
WHEN GOD'S PEOPLE PRAY

And when they had prayed, the place where they were

assembled together was shaken; and they were all

filled with the Holy Spirit, and they spoke

the Word of God with boldness.

(Acts 4:31)

INTRODUCTION

Do you know what happens when you pray? Do you know that you have been given power and authority by Jesus Christ? Before you can begin to understand what prayer can do or what happens when God's people pray, you need to believe in the Word of God. The Bible is our starting point. Jesus told the Sadducees:

> "You are in error because you do not know the Scriptures or the power of God." *(Matthew 22:29)*

Many of us only resort to praying when tragedy strikes. Serious prayer is usually driven by necessity. Prayer has become a 'spare tire'. We only remember it when we get a 'flat'. Is it possible that we don't pray because we don't understand the power of prayer? I hear people say, "We've done all we can. The only thing we can do now is pray." Or: "When all else fails – pray!" But our best efforts must begin with prayer. Prayer should be our first response rather than our last resort.

The church is constantly devising new methods and new plans to grow and spread the gospel. This trend of the day has a tendency to lose sight of the man or sink the man in the plan or organization. God's plan is to make much of the man, far more of him than of anything else. Men are God's method. The Church is looking for better methods; God is looking for better men. What the Church needs today is not more machinery or better methods but better men and women of prayer, like Elijah. The Bible says in James 5:17-18 that:

> "Elijah was a man with a nature like ours, and he prayed earnestly that it would not rain; and it did not rain on the land for three years and six months. And he prayed again, and the heaven gave rain, and the earth produced its fruit".

Our greatest need today is powerful, persistent, passionate, prevailing prayer. The need is far greater than most of us realize.

God most definitely listens to prayers, answers prayers, and moves in response to prayers. Jesus taught:

> "...I tell you the truth, if you have faith as small as a mustard seed, you can say to this mountain, 'Move from here to there' and it will move. Nothing will be impossible for you." *(Matthew 17:20)*

And 2 Corinthians 10:4-5 tells us that:

> "The weapons we fight with are not the weapons of the world. On the contrary, they have divine power to demolish strongholds. We demolish arguments and every pretension that sets itself up against the knowledge of God, and we take captive every thought to make it obedient to Christ." *(NIV)*

My prayer is that this book will deepen your understanding of the power of prayer. I pray that you will become certain of what happens when you, a child of the Living God, pray. I pray that you will receive clarity on the things in your life that are hindering your prayers and address them. I pray that you will be moved to cry out in intercession for your loved ones and the lost. I pray that you will be confident in your prayers. I pray that you will move mountains, reach the lost, witness to nations and fulfill God's perfect plan and purpose for your life.

CHAPTER ONE

WHAT DOES PRAYER DO?

The original Greek word for prayer is *"proseuche,"* which means communion with God. Prayer is our direct line with heaven. To many people prayer seems complicated, but it is simple, it is talking to God. Cell phones and other devices have become a necessity to most people in society today. We have Bluetooth devices, iPhones, and even talking computers! These are means of communication that allow two or more people to interact, discuss, and respond to one another. Prayer is the means of communication that allows us to do all those things with God.

Prayer for some of us has become a cliché. People often say, "You are in our prayers". What does that mean? They mean you are in their thoughts. But being in my thoughts doesn't necessarily mean I am praying for you. When you share a concern, some may respond and say, "I'm going to pray for you". But most people don't pray for you. Anytime someone says "I'm going to pray for you," I say "Why don't you pray for me right now, because I know you are not actually going to pray for me".

We don't pray because we don't understand the power of prayer. Prayer is connecting with God. It is exercising authority over principalities. God created mankind with the ability to exercise authority upon the earth. In the New Testament we are taught that prayer gives us this privilege. Through prayer we are causing things in heaven to happen on earth.

Prayer changes things. Men and women in the Bible changed the course of history because of their prayers. Again, James 5:17 says:

> "Elijah was a man with a nature like ours, and he prayed earnestly that it would not rain; and it did not rain on the land for three years and six months."

This means it doesn't take an extraordinary person to cause things to happen. It doesn't matter who you are or where you come from, you can change situations with your prayers. How do you respond, for example, if the doctor says that you are so sick and that there is nothing that he can do about it? Are you going to say, "Well, I guess there is nothing else to do but pray?" Hello? Nothing else to do but pray? Is prayer your last resort or your first response? My hope and my prayer is that after reading this book, something in your spirit will shift, and that prayer will become your most important weapon.

Jesus said in Matthew 22:29:

> "You are mistaken, not knowing the Scriptures or the power of God."

The reason we don't pray is because we don't understand, not only the scriptures, but the power of God.

Let me give a few insights to help you understand why your prayer is critical.

PRAYER PRODUCES PASSION

Humankind's deepest longing is to connect with God. Prayer gives us the opportunity to fulfill that longing. Jesus says in Mark 12:29-30:

> "...the first of all the commandments is: 'Hear, O Israel, the Lord our God, the Lord is one. And you shall love the Lord your God with all your heart, with all your soul, with all your mind, and with all your strength'."

Jesus said this is the greatest of all, this is above all. This loving with everything you have creates intimacy. It creates a passion for the things of God.

Why is it so important to connect with God in intimacy? Because that is where we are most fulfilled! Sex, drugs, alcohol, and material things cannot fulfill us; those are temporary pleasures that do not have a lasting impact on your level of fulfillment.

Loving God makes it easier to love other people. God's love connects us. When we experience the passion of God, He touches our hearts and we can touch other people. You can even hang out and worship with people you don't want to worship with. In fact black, white, yellow and brown people are meant to worship together. Jesus said in Mark 11:17:

> "Is it not written, 'My house shall be called a house of prayer for all nations…'?"

Unfortunately, as Martin Luther said, *"Sunday morning has become the most segregated hour of the week"*. Most people go to church based on the color of their skin. They will not worship with a neighbor who has a different skin color. The church is the only institution where people gather based on the color of their skin. This blatant segregation based on the colour of skin isn't allowed anywhere, so why is the church getting away with it? When we love God, He gives us the ability to love others also. When we love God, we are able to see people and situations the way that He does.

When we love God, we are able to obey His commandments. In John 14:23 Jesus says:

> "If anyone loves Me, he will keep My word; and My Father will love him, and We will come to him and make Our home with him."

What is Jesus talking about? Obeying God begins with loving God. Have you wondered why you struggle to obey God? It is because there is no intimacy. That's why it all begins with prayer. When I come to God in prayer I am building intimacy so as to become everything that God has created me to be. When I get connected with God, I am able to be fulfilled, I am able to love others and I am able to obey His commandments.

PRAYER PRODUCES PURITY

Prayer gives us the opportunity as a child of God to get a fresh start. Because we are not perfect we need to stay in purity in order to fulfill our destiny. Prayer gives us the opportunity to receive cleansing for our sins. How do you confess your sins if you don't pray? Prayer gives you the opportunity to say "God, I know I've done some stuff. Some of it I know, some of it I don't even know". 1 John 1:9 says:

> "If we confess our sins, He is faithful and just to forgive us our sins and to cleanse us from all unrighteousness."

The power of God is able to cleanse you, wash you and justify you. When we enter into prayer we can claim the blood of Jesus Christ upon ourselves. I like what the Bible says in Hebrews 10:19-22:

> "Therefore, brethren, having boldness to enter the Holiest by the blood of Jesus, by a new and living way which He consecrated for us, through the veil, that is, His flesh, and having a High Priest over the house of God, let us draw near with a true heart in full assurance of faith, having our hearts sprinkled from an evil conscience and our bodies washed with pure water."

To understand the power of cleansing you must understand the power of the tabernacle. In the Old Testament, not everyone could come into the Presence of God. It was only the high priest who could come to God's presence once every year. But because of the death of Christ we now have the privilege of coming to His presence anytime!

Some of us do not come boldly before God because we are afraid, or sometimes we think we are not worthy. We are not sure how God is going to treat us. But the Bible says that because of the blood of the lamb, we can stand holy and pure before God. It doesn't matter how others see you. Come boldly into God's presence and say "Daddy, we need to hang out." The Bible says:

> "The wicked flee when no one pursues, but the righteous are bold as a lion." *(Proverbs 28:1)*

I come boldly before God. When I stand before God, I speak confidently because I know where I stand. Not even the devil can accuse me of any sin because I know my sins have been forgiven and washed by the blood of the lamb.

PRAYER PRODUCES POWER

Power for Service: If we are going to do what God has called us to do, we need power. Power comes through prayer. Show me a child of God who has power and I will show you a child of God who prays. Show me a powerless Christian and I will show you a prayerless Christian. Power comes through prayer. Jesus told the disciples they would receive power from on high when the Holy Spirit came upon them (Acts 1:8). Again, Acts 4:31 says:

> "And when they had prayed, the place where they were assembled together was shaken; and they were all filled with the Holy Spirit, and they spoke the word of God with boldness."

Power over Sin: Prayer will break the cycle of sin in your life! Psalm 40:1-3 says:

> "I waited patiently for the Lord; and He inclined to me, and heard my cry. He also brought me up out of a horrible pit, out of the miry clay, and set my feet upon a rock, and established my steps. He has put a new song in my mouth—praise to our God. Many will see it and fear, and will trust in the Lord."

That's what prayer can do. It will bring you out of that miry clay that keeps you stuck in the same sin. I mean that same sin that you have been committing over and over again. Talk to the Lord. Wait on the Lord. He will set you free.

I know of a man called Jacob in the Bible. He was born blessed. He smelled blessed. But he never lived a blessed life. Throughout his life he was a deceiver. He was a mess! He had to fight for everything. Until one day he got sick and tired of living a second-class life. He went into prayer. He told his wife and children, "There is something I have to do but I have to do it alone". All night he wrestled with God until God changed him. I don't know what you are struggling with, but I know that prayer can set you free.

PRAYER PRODUCES PEACE

Why are we so stressed and anxious in our society? I believe it is because we are not praying. I can't tell you how many times I've stood in a bus stop with nothing in my pocket while knowing I must get from point A to point B. One day

I was invited to speak at a conference but had no money. I stood at the bus stop believing that if God had sent me then He would provide me with transportation. And He did. Someone stopped to tell me he had a strong urge to give me ride. That was God. Philippians 4:6-7 says:

> "Be anxious for nothing, but in everything by prayer and supplication, with thanksgiving, let your requests be made known to God; and the peace of God, which surpasses all understanding, will guard your hearts and minds through Christ Jesus."

Right there is the best medication for anxiety. It is not prescription drugs. It is prayer. Prayer causes God's peace to guard your mind and heart. Prayer causes you to focus on God and His promises. Worry causes you to focus on your life and its problems. Big difference. Isaiah 26:3-4 says:

> "You will keep him in perfect peace, whose mind is stayed on You, because he trusts in You. Trust in the Lord forever, for in YAHWEH, the Lord, is everlasting strength."

PRAYER PRODUCES PURPOSE

Acts 9:6 says:

> "So he, trembling and astonished, said, 'Lord, what do You want me to do?' Then the Lord said to him, 'Arise and go into the city, and you will be told what you must do'."

Do you want to know God's purpose and destiny for your

life? You have to pray. Paul prayed. You need to ask: "God, why am I here?" He will tell you. God will show you. There are lots of Christians today in the church who don't know God's purpose for their lives. Do you know why you are here on earth? Ask God! Sometimes you may need to take a three day fast and seek His face. Without His answer you will live without knowing your purpose, and a life without purpose leads to a life of frustration.

PRAYER PRODUCES PROVISION

Mathew 7:7-11 says:

> "Ask, and it will be given to you; seek, and you will find; knock, and it will be opened to you. For everyone who asks receives, and he who seeks finds, and to him who knocks it will be opened. Or what man is there among you who, if his son asks for bread, will give him a stone? Or if he asks for a fish, will he give him a serpent? If you then, being evil, know how to give good gifts to your children, how much more will your Father who is in heaven give good things to those who ask Him!"

Again Psalm 50:15 says:

> "Call upon Me in the day of trouble; I will deliver you, and you shall glorify Me."

You know what God is saying? "My glory is at stake here". So child of God "Call upon Me!" How can we go to the world and tell about God's goodness when we haven't experienced it? He brought Israel out of Egypt *"... by His mighty hand"* so that the world may know that He is a powerful God. He shows us signs and wonders and miracles to show us that He is alive.

When the man who had been crippled all his life was healed, he began to dance and glorify God. Nobody told him, "Now is the time to worship." No!! The Bible says he immediately began to jump on his feet and dance. Then some of the Pharisees asked him, "What about this man, do you really know about him? Do you know that He is a sinner?" But the blind man responded, "I don't know if He is a sinner or not, all I know is that I was blind and now I can see" *(John 9)*. We need testimony of God's provision to show a doubting world that Jesus is alive.

PRAYER PRODUCES PERSEVERANCE

Prayer will never let you give up! It produces the strength and stamina you need to keep going. I have never been "burnt out." You cannot "burn out" as long as you pray. Prayer ushers you into God's presence...which produces fresh power. Isaiah 40:28-31 says:

> "Have you not known? Have you not heard? The ever-lasting God, the Lord, the Creator of the ends of the earth, neither faints nor is weary. His understanding is unsearchable. He gives power to the weak, and to those who have no might He increases strength. Even the youths shall faint and be weary, and the young men shall utterly fall, but those who wait on the Lord shall re-

new their strength; They shall mount up with wings like eagles, they shall run and not be weary, they shall walk and not faint. Seek the Lord! He will be your strength and a strong tower!"

CHAPTER TWO

HINDRANCES TO PRAYER

If God hears our prayers, how come some of them go unanswered? 1 Peter 3:7 says:

> "Husbands, likewise, dwell with them with understanding, giving honor to the wife, as to the weaker vessel, and as being heirs together of the grace of life, that your prayers may not be hindered."

This passage makes it clear that, although God answers prayers, our prayers can be hindered based on our attitude and our actions. This particular passage is talking about how husbands have to treat their wives in a certain way, because the way they relate to their wives can affect how their prayers are answered. In this chapter, I am going to focus on seven of the hindrances to prayer.

UNCONFESSED SIN

We know that sin can block our prayers. Psalm 66:18 says, *"If I regard iniquity in my heart the Lord will not hear"*. Iniquity is a sin in our life that has come to remain. The sin we have not confessed. Sin blocks our fellowship with God. Sin also blocks our blessings. Isaiah 59:1-2 says:

> "Behold, the Lord's hand is not shortened, that it cannot save; nor His ear heavy, that it cannot hear. But your iniquities have separated you from your God; and your sins have hidden His face from you, so that He will not hear."

Never allow sin to stay in your life. Confess your sins as soon as the Holy Spirit convicts you.

UNBELIEVING HEART

An unbelieving heart blocks our prayers. Faith is crucial to our relationship with God. Hebrews 11:6 says:

> "But without faith it is impossible to please Him, for he who comes to God must believe that He is, and that He is a rewarder of those who diligently seek Him."

And in James 1:5-8 we read:

> "If any of you lacks wisdom, let him ask of God, who gives to all liberally and without reproach, and it will be given to him. But let him ask in faith, with no doubting, for he who doubts is like a wave of the sea driven and tossed by the wind. For let not that man suppose that he will receive anything from the Lord; he is a double-minded man, unstable in all his ways."

Jesus says in Mark 11:22, *"Have faith in God"*. We need to come into the presence of God in faith. I believe the reason some of our prayers are not answered is that we don't really believe that God can answer our prayers. Our faith must be founded on these three things:

1. God's Promises

What He says, He will do. He cannot lie. Numbers 23:19 says:

> "God is not a man, that He should lie, nor a son of man, that He should repent. Has He said, and will He not do? Or has He spoken, and will He not make it good?"

God is greater than your father, mother, or your boss. When he says He will do it, He will. What He has promised He will fulfill. He has the capacity to do so. I promised my daughter some time ago that I would take her out on a date, but then I forgot about it. I forgot because I am human. But God cannot forget because He is God. Isaiah 49:15-16 says:

> "Can a woman forget her nursing child and not have compassion on the son of her womb? Surely they may forget, Yet I will not forget you. See, I have inscribed you on the palms of My hands; Your walls are continually before Me."

2. God's Power

The one who has promised is able. I can promise to give you $5000, but I may not have the ability to give you the money. My promises are limited because I am limited. But God is all powerful! The Bible says He created the whole world by His Word. He spoke and it came into being. When God gives me a promise I know He has the ability to fulfill it. He is able because He's all-powerful. If God has promised you something and that thing doesn't exist, don't worry. Wal-mart or any other store may not have it but that does not mean God cannot supply. Philippians 4:19 says:

> "And my God shall supply all your needs according to His riches in glory by Christ Jesus."

Remember, God's supply does not depend on Wal-Mart, but "according to His riches in glory". If God has promised you a husband and there are no husbands left on this planet, don't worry. He has the power to create one just for you. When God promised Adam a wife, there were no women. So He created a woman for him. God does not need our limited resources in order to provide for us. When the experts say the job market is limited, some of us become discouraged. But our faith is not rooted in expert opinion. When God says He is going to give you a job, it means if there is none, He will create one for you. I have heard several testimonies from people who have had positions created just for them. What God has promised you He also has the power to deliver.

3. *God's Past Performance*

Many things, including economic predictions, are based on past performance. Our ability to get a particular job or enter an educational institute is based on our past performance. Similarly, God's track record is an important indicator of what He is going to do in the future. I am totally encouraged when I look at God's work as recorded in the Bible. I am able to see all His fulfilled promises. This is where faith is rooted. When people were hungry, as promised, He fed them. When people were sick, as promised, He healed them. When people needed signs and wonders, as promised, He provided them. Romans 4:18-21 says:

> "Against all hope, Abraham in hope believed and so became the father of many nations, just as it had been said to him, 'So shall your offspring be.' Without weakening in his faith, he faced the fact that his body was as good as dead—since he was about a hundred years old—and that Sarah's womb was also dead. Yet he did not waver through unbelief regarding the promise of God, but was strengthened in his faith and gave glory to God, being fully persuaded that God had power to do what He had promised." *(NIV)*

Abraham's faith was not rooted in thin air. It was rooted on God's past performances. Like creating the world out of nothing. Like sustaining Noah and His family in the ark for forty days. Romans 10:17 says, *"So then faith cometh by hearing and hearing the Word of God."* When I read God's Word and see what God has done in the past, it stirs up faith in me. David believed he could kill Goliath because his faith was rooted in God's past performance. This is what he said:

> "The Lord who rescued me from the paw of the lion and the paw of the bear will rescue me from the hand of this Philistine.' and Saul said to David, 'Go, and the Lord be with you'." *(1 Samuel 17:37)*

Every testimony you have, even the ones that seem small, deepen the roots of your faith and enable you to do mighty things. The God that protected you against that accident or that poor decision, can also save your marriage.

When you pray, you need to stand on God's past performance. Do you remember the story of Jesus feeding the five thousand? The Bible says that afterwards they went into a boat and were beset by a bad storm. They began to complain and doubt:

> "For they had not understood about the loaves, because their heart was hardened." *(Mark 6:52)*

Never forget God's past performance. If you feel God has done nothing for you in the past, get into His Word. The Bible is rich with examples of God's promises and His fulfillment of them.

In our culture we depend so much on what we can see, what we can feel, and what we can touch. I am here to tell you there is a world out there which you cannot see or touch. There is a world out there you cannot experience with your human senses. We call it the "sixth sense", because it falls outside the five commonly understood senses of seeing, hearing, touching, tasting and smelling. You need to tap into that "sixth sense". The fact that I cannot see something does not mean it does not exist. Because someone says it is impossible doesn't mean that God cannot work a miracle. In fact a miracle is not a miracle until we see it as impossible. The impossibility should not cause doubt, but be an opportunity to see God perform a miracle.

Doctors may tell you that you have only three months to live. But that is only a medical opinion. You need to also seek God's opinion. If He says you will live, then stand on His Word because He has the final say! Any doctor who might have examined Abraham and Sarah would have concluded that they could never have children. Both were too old. But God had already told Abraham that he was going to be a father of nations.

As a child of God, you are going to face situations where no human can help you. You need to build your faith now because there will come a time when you are going to need it. The problem with many of us in "advanced" societies is that we have come to depend on systems instead of God. What happens when the system fails or is unable to help us? There will come a time when you are sick and no amount of medical care can help you. The system is limited but God is unlimited! That is why Abraham never wavered in faith. He trusted in God's promise because of God's past performance.

Because we have been disappointed by people in the past we may think God too will disappoint us. God is not like us. He is almighty, omnipresent, and omnipotent. The idea of growing in faith begins with the understanding that God is bigger than your situation and bigger than any human system. Jesus came upon Peter at the seaside where he had fished all night but caught nothing. But He told Peter to cast his net into the deep (Luke 5:4). To which Peter replied, *"Master, we have toiled all night and caught nothing" (Luke 5:5)*. Peter's response was founded on his earthly problem and circumstances, on a faulty system. We must not allow failure of our systems to keep us from seeking our miracles today.

You need to believe God's Word for you right now and run with it! When the woman with the issue of blood met Jesus, we know from the Bible that she had a bad history. There were people who promised to help her receive healing, they took her money and didn't help her. But she learned how to forget her grief and disappointment. The Bible says:

> "When she heard about Jesus, she came behind Him in the crowd and touched His garment. For she said, 'If only I may touch His clothes, I shall be made well.' Immediately the fountain of her blood was dried up, and she felt in her body that she was healed of the affliction." *(Mark 5:27-29)*

Forget about any negative past experiences and trust in God's past performance.

UNFORGIVING ATTITUDE

We all go through situations that wound us deeply. And as long as you are involved in human relationships, you are going to get hurt. We cannot control what people do or say. But we can control how we respond. We are expected to respond in the way His Word leads us. It is clear, your prayers will not be answered if you hold grudges. Jesus put it powerfully in Matthew 5:23-24:

> "Therefore if you bring your gift to the altar, and there remember that your brother has something against you, leave your gift there before the altar, and go your way. First be reconciled to your brother, and then come and offer your gift."

This can apply to your husband, your wife, your friend or anybody who has grieved you. The Bible says stop. Go and forgive first!

In Matthew 6:14-15, Jesus also says:

> "For if you forgive other people when they sin against you, your heavenly Father will also forgive you. But if you do not forgive others their sins, your Father will not forgive your sins." *(NIV)*

God will not listen to us when we harbor unforgiveness. I know forgiveness is never easy, especially when the wounds are deep. But unforgiveness is not an option. It messes us up and it blocks our prayers.

UNACCEPTABLE REQUEST

Something else that can block our prayers is unacceptable requests. The Bible says we have to pray according to the will of God to receive answers to our prayers. We have to align our hearts with God's heart. 1 John 5:14 says:

> "This is the confidence we have in approaching God: that if we ask anything according to His will, He hears us." *(NIV)*

How do I know the will of God? First, His Word. If I ask anything according to what He has said in His Word I know He will hear me. For example, I know what God says about my provision. The Bible says He will supply all my needs. So I come to God in confidence knowing what His Word says about my needs. Sometimes we know what God's Word says but we try to convince Him to change it. I know what God's Word says about the kind of person I can marry. For example, a believer cannot marry a non-believer. And yet we come to God saying, "Lord I know the Bible says I cannot marry a non-believer but this one is a different kind of non-believer. He doesn't go to church but he is good, his heart is clean." God will not answer a prayer like that. He will not go against His Word.

Second, you can know the will of God through the Holy Spirit. When we are praying about something outside of God's will, the Holy Spirit will check our heart. We may experience, for example, restlessness in our heart when we are praying for our own selfish reason. James 4:3 says:

> "When you ask, you do not receive, because you ask with wrong motives, that you may spend what you get on your pleasures." *(NIV)*

You need to ask yourself, for example, "Why do I want to buy a new house?" Is it because you just visited someone with a nice home and you are coveting what they have? Your kitchen was great, until you visited someone with a nicer kitchen, and now yours seems lacking. God will not answer selfish prayers. Ask the Holy Spirit to check your motives.

UNSEEN FORCES

Our prayers can also be hindered by unseen forces. Daniel 10:12-14 describes this scenario:

> "Do not be afraid, Daniel. Since the first day that you set your mind to gain understanding and to humble yourself before your God, your words were heard, and I have come in response to them. But the prince of the Persian kingdom resisted me twenty-one days. Then Michael, one of the chief princes, came to help me, because I was detained there with the king of Persia. Now I have come to explain to you what will happen to your people in the future, for the vision concerns a time yet to come." *(NIV)*

Daniel's prayer was heard and answered the very day he prayed. But there was an unseen force that wanted to make sure that Daniel did not receive the answer to his prayers. The battle was so intense that the angel had to call for a backup. That is why, child of God, you don't give up when you are praying. Keep pushing and pressing in, until you experience a breakthrough. Something could be blocking your prayer in the atmosphere, but you must learn to persist!

Sometimes we may blame God for unanswered prayers without understanding what is going on in the Spirit realm. There could spiritual blockages. I love Jesus' parable in Luke 18:1-8:

> "One day Jesus told his disciples a story to show that they should always pray and never give up, "'There was a judge in a certain city,' He said, 'who neither feared God nor cared about people. A widow of that city came to him repeatedly, saying, "Give me justice in this dispute with my enemy." The judge ignored her for a while, but finally he said to himself, 'I don't fear God or care about people, but this woman is driving me crazy. I'm going to see that she gets justice, because she is wearing me out with her constant requests!' Then the Lord said, 'Learn a lesson from this unjust judge. Even he rendered a just decision in the end. So don't you think God will surely give justice to his chosen people who cry out to him day and night? Will he keep putting them off? I tell you, he will grant justice to them quickly! But when the Son of Man returns, how many will he find on the earth who have faith'?" *(NLT)*

Do you catch what is happening here? This unjust judge refuses to answer the woman's request but her consistent prayers began to wear him out. Anytime you discern that your prayers are being blocked by unseen forces, keep pressing in.

UNSUITABLE TIMING

Sometimes our prayers are hindered because the timing is

not right. Habakkuk 2:3 says:

> "For the vision is yet for an appointed time; but at the end it will speak, and it will not lie. Though it tarries, wait for it; because it will surely come, it will not tarry."

Timing is important when it comes to the things of the kingdom of God. Abraham had to wait for twenty-five years before his prayer for a child was answered. Joseph had to wait for more than seventeen years before being released from jail. David had to wait for years before being crowned as king. That's why it is good to wait upon God. Wait for that job. Wait for that husband. Wait for that healing. David said:

> "I waited patiently for the Lord to help me and He turned to me and heard my cry. He lifted me out of the pit of despair, out of the mud and the mire. He set my feet on solid ground and steadied me as I walked along. He has given me a new song to sing, hymn of praise to our God. Many will see what he has done and be amazed. They will put their trust in the Lord." *(Psalm 40:1-3; NLT)*

UNKNOWN REASONS

Finally, sometimes our prayers are hindered for reasons we may never know. I am sorry to disappoint you, but there are unanswered prayers that you will not understand until we get to heaven. I call this the sovereignty of God. There are just some things we don't know.

Sometimes it's just purely for the glory of God. 2 Corinthians 12:8-10 tells us about Paul's experience with this:

> "Three times I pleaded with the Lord to take it away from me. But he said to me, 'My grace is sufficient for you, for My power is made perfect in weakness.' Therefore I will boast all the more gladly about my weaknesses, so that Christ's power may rest on me. That is why, for Christ's sake, I delight in weaknesses, in insults, in hardships, in persecutions, in difficulties. For when I am weak, then I am strong." *(NIV)*

Paul prayed and prayed but God simply said, "My grace is sufficient for you". God did not answer his prayer but gave him the grace to go through his circumstance.

There may be situations in your life that have no business being there. You have prayed and done everything and God simply says, "My grace is sufficient." You may not understand everything about your situation, but keep praising Him anyway. Habakkuk 3:17-19 says:

> "Though the fig tree does not bud and there are no grapes on the vines, though the olive crop fails and the fields produce no food, though there are no sheep in the pen and no cattle in the stalls, yet I will rejoice in the Lord, I will be joyful in God my Savior. The Sovereign Lord is my strength; he makes my feet like the feet of a deer, he enables me to tread on the heights." *(NIV)*

CHAPTER THREE

KINDS OF PRAYER

We have been talking about what prayer is and the things that can hinder its fulfillment. Now we are going into deeper territory to talk about how to take our prayer to a different level. In Ephesians 6:18 Paul says:

> "Pray in the Spirit on all occasions with all kinds of prayers." *(NIV)*

What are the kinds of prayers? We don't just pray one particular way all the time, there are many kinds of prayers and every prayer is made for a different occasion. Some of us pray the same way at all times on all occasions. That is not effective! What Paul is saying is that if we are going to overcome, if we are going to win the battle before us, we have to pray all kinds of prayers. Prayers are like keys. There are certain keys you use only for certain doors. In this chapter we are going to deal with five kinds of prayer.

UNCEASING PRAYER

Unceasing prayer is simply praying all the time. 1 Thessalonians 5:17; *"Pray without ceasing"*. It is becoming constantly aware of and flowing with the presence of God. This kind of prayer will transform your life. If at every moment of your life you are connected with the presence of Jesus, it is certain to change the way you are living.

This is not like waking up in the morning and spending a quiet time with the Lord. It is beyond that. Some people don't have a devotional life. They just pray on the run. Unceasing prayer assumes you have prayed in the morning or in the evening, and spent your quiet time with the Lord. Quiet time prepares and moves you into the realm of unceasing prayer. Some people call it 'walking in the Spirit'. I call it 'spiritual breathing'. It is like the way you breathe in and breathe out all the time. In the middle of the day? Say a prayer. Facing a client? Say a prayer. On a journey? Say a prayer. God brings someone to mind? Say a prayer. You are in constant connection with heaven.

There are two primary benefits of unceasing prayer. First, it makes you alert to the voice of God. God wants to speak to you all the time, but sometimes you are not listening. When you are engaged in unceasing prayer you become sensitive to the voice of God. Something tugs your heart to make a choice, even to take a particular bridge. God is trying to reach you. It could be an accident or a situation that God is trying to protect you from. Unceasing prayer opens your spirit to receive the Holy Spirit. Many times we are so distracted that when God is knocking and seeking and speaking we cannot hear him. Position yourself in a way that you can hear the voice of God. He wants to speak to you. Prayer is a two-way conversation. You speak to God and He speaks to you.

Jesus did that all the time. How many times did we see Jesus in the midst of preaching or ministering and He stops to pray? On one occasion, as He was teaching *(John chapter 12)*, all of sudden He said; *"Glorify your name"* and then a voice came up and said *"I have glorified it, and will glorify it again" (John 12:28)*. It is interesting that the people around Jesus heard, not God's voice, but thunder. It is the same in church. God could be speaking to you in church, but everyone else would just be hearing noise. They are tuned out. In other words, God will speak but only those that are tuned to His voice will hear Him, the rest just hear noise.

The second benefit of unceasing prayer is that it makes you alert to Satan's works. His primary modus operandi is setting traps. 1 Peter 5:8 says:

> "Be sober, be vigilant; because your adversary the devil walks about like a roaring lion, seeking whom he may devour."

Unceasing prayer places you in that place where you become aware of his schemes.

Don't wait for your world to fall apart before you call upon God. As you move through your day, remember the Bible teaches us to walk in the Spirit so you will not fulfill the lusts of flesh (Galatians 5:16). Sometimes you need to confess your sin on the spot. You have said something that is not right....right away you pray and you talk to God. Sometimes you need to ask Him for strength to deal with particular circumstances: You are in a conversation or a situation that is not going well. You can ask God to guide your lips.

Unceasing prayer means that throughout the day God is touching your heart and the Holy Spirit is bringing thoughts to your mind. God is doing things in your soul. This is one kind of prayer that will carry you through your day. Our days are filled with busyness, distraction and stress. You are going through life's journey and travail but you stop a moment and whisper a prayer. You say thank you to Jesus or remember something God has done for you. Try this for the next six weeks. Staying in constant prayer. Anything you do continuously for six weeks becomes a habit. Start this holy habit.

INTERCESSORY PRAYER

The second kind of prayer is intercessory prayer. Here we shift prayer from our own needs to the needs of others. It is selfless and self-giving. Every child of God needs to enter into intercession. It is critical for the salvation of the world and for your family. It is part of who we are as children of God.

When we enter into intercessory prayer we are entering a

priestly ministry. The primary function of a priest is to intercede, to stand in between God and the people. Jesus Christ is our high priest and the Bible says He intercedes for us. The Holy Spirit also intercedes for us. So in intercessory prayer we join God in the ministry of standing in the gap for other people.

You need to step up your prayer life from pleading for your own needs, problems and desires; to praying for other people's needs, dreams, issues, and burdens. Begin to wake up in the middle of the night to plead on behalf of somebody. It is part of our calling. In the book of Genesis we are told about God visiting Abraham. He was wondering whether or not to tell Abraham what was going to happen to Sodom and Gomorrah. This is because He knew that Abraham would begin to intercede. And when God finally told Abraham, of course, immediately Abraham entered into intercession *(Genesis 18)*. Abraham knew no-one except Lot and his family in Sodom. Why was he pleading for people he did not know? What would you do? If God comes to your city and says He is going to destroy it, will you stand in the gap for it or let Him destroy it? God loves sinners, just as He loves you. He cares for people. When people say things like "I hope the homosexuals will burn in hell," they don't have the heart of Jesus. If you have the heart of Jesus and you know somebody is not living a particular way, you will cry out for them, fast for them and plead for them. Do you have the heart of Christ?

Abraham negotiated with God and said, "...what if there is ten righteous, then will you spare Sodom?" Like Abraham, an intercessor knows how to negotiate. Begin to intercede for your children. Negotiate with God for your daughters, plead for your sons, call on God on their behalf. When you stand in the gap you are fulfilling your priestly role. The Bible says that Job would rise up every morning and intercede for his children, make sacrifices for them and plead for them. Are you aware that you are the high priest in your house? Do you know that you need to stand in the gap so that the devil will not mess up the minds of your children? Plead for your children from the moment they are in the womb, that they will love and seek God, and that no weapon formed against them shall prosper. Then begin to pray for your community, your city, your country and your continent. Pray that God will have mercy.

Remember again that intercession is selfless and self-giving. Moses was an intercessor. True intercession is not about oneself. In Exodus 32:9-10 God told Moses:

> "I have seen these people, and behold, it is a stiff-necked people. Now therefore let Me alone, that My wrath may wax hot against them and that I may consume them: and I will make thee a great nation."

God was going destroy everybody but make Moses great. How would you have reacted? This is how Moses reacted, he sought the favor of the Lord his God:

> "'Lord,' he said, 'why should your anger burn against

your people, whom you brought out of Egypt with great power and a mighty hand? Why should the Egyptians say, "It was with evil intent that he brought them out, to kill them in the mountains and to wipe them off the face of the earth?" Turn from your fierce anger; relent and do not bring disaster on your people. Remember your servants Abraham, Isaac and Israel, to whom You swore by your own self: 'I will make your descendants as numerous as the stars in the sky and I will give your descendants all this land I promised them, and it will be their inheritance forever.' Then the Lord relented and did not bring on his people the disaster he had threatened." *(Exodus 32:11-14)*

The intercessor will place personal ambition and agendas aside and hold people in prayer for God's name's sake.

As you can see from the above Scripture, Moses appealed to God's Word and promise. The true intercessor knows the Word of God, and they know how to stand on it in prayer. They never forget what the Word of the Lord says and they hold fast to it in prayer. God loves people who can stand on His promises and remind Him of His Word. He is not intimidated by it. The Bible says "The Lord relented..." Why? Because somebody stood in the gap and said "No". Somebody stood in the gap and held back the anger of God. God is calling on us to take our prayer life to the next level of intercession.

I remember a few years ago the Lord woke me one night to pray for Bangladesh. I said "Bangla-what?? Lord, why are you waking me up to pray for a place I don't even know or care about?" But I obeyed Him. And two days later Bangladesh experienced a terrible flood. I believe it could have been worse. God was looking for men and women to stand in the gap. God may wake you up one day and say "pray for a missionary in China", or "pray for a missionary in Russia". You have to position yourself at that place where God can trust you with His burden. If He knows you are a true intercessor, He will trust you with events, He will trust you with people, He will trust you with names, He will trust you with countries. He will trust you with things He is planning to do or what the enemy's plans are. Can you stand in the gap and pray? Can God trust you with a disaster knowing that you will stand and pray?

Sometimes we are caught up with our own petty prayers like "Lord give me an iPhone..." when souls are perishing. We pray "gimme gimme" prayers when God is saying, "Forget about yourselves and pray for nations, kingdoms and principalities and cities". He's asking you to pray for a wife and husband who are about to break up the following morning. Can God trust you to honor that request? Ezekiel 22:29 makes it clear that when there is sin in the land, God will always look for intercessors. If our city is destroyed, will it be because God could not find intercessors?

1 Timothy 2:1-2 says:

> "I urge, then, first of all, that petitions, prayers, intercession and thanksgiving be made for all peo-

ple—for kings and all those in authority, that we may live peaceful and quiet lives in all godliness and holiness." *(NIV)*

You see, there is residual benefit in standing in the gap. Moreover, as we stand in the gap for others, God will take care of our own. Job 42:10 says:

"And the Lord turned the captivity of Job, when he prayed for his friends." *(KJV)*

AUTHORITATIVE PRAYER

Authoritative prayer is when we exercise our God-given authority to overcome situations. In normal prayer you talk to God. In authoritative prayer you talk for God. It is not directed to God. You exercise the authority God has given you in situations. You are commanding what God has already commanded. There are some things that God will not do for us. It is like when you ask God to move a mountain. He has already given you the authority to move the mountain yourself! When Jesus Christ came across someone who was possessed He was not asking God to help Him overcome the demon, but rather He spoke to the demon and said "be quiet and come out". You and I have the authority to do that. God has given us the keys to exercise that authority. Jesus spoke to the wind and said, "...*wind be still*".

There is a difference between power and authority. In authority you speak directly to circumstance. Authority is when you begin to express the power that God has given you. There is a power outlet in the wall and there is a beautiful fan, but both are useless if the fan is not plugged into the outlet. This is where some children of God are limited. We have been given so much but we are not tapping in. There are times when you must speak directly to situations in your family, your business, and your marriage. Luke 9:1 says, "Then He called His twelve disciples together and gave them power and authority over all demons, and to cure diseases". This is what God has given you. We don't need to say "God help me to overcome, help me to move this or that." God says "I have given you the authority". If you travel and leave your child with a credit card for their needs, they don't call you to say they are hungry. They use the card to buy food. In the same way, why call on God for things He has already given us?

There is a difference between one who is exercising his authority and one who is not. A police officer who is off duty does not have the same authority as one in uniform and on duty. God has given you that uniform. The problem is that the devil knows we have the uniform but we don't use the authority that comes with it. Many of us don't understand it. We don't grasp it. So we live a defeated lifestyle and Satan is happy to see us in our ignorance. Whenever a child of God says "in the name of Jesus" the enemy is afraid, because we are wearing our uniform and wielding our authority.

Matthew 16:18-19 says:

> "And I also say to you that you are Peter, and on this rock I will build My church, and the gates of Hades shall not prevail against it. And I will give you the keys of the kingdom of heaven, and whatever you bind on earth will be bound in heaven, and whatever you loose on earth will be loosed in heaven."

We have the same keys to the kingdom. Use them. Whatever you bind in heaven shall be bound on earth, whatever you loose in heaven shall be loosed on earth. When you cause things to close they will close, when you cause them to open they will open. That is authoritative prayer.

In Exodus 14:15-16 God says to Moses:

> "Why do you cry to Me? Tell the children of Israel to go forward. But lift up your rod, and stretch out your hand over the sea and divide it. And the children of Israel shall go on dry ground through the midst of the sea."

Moses knew he had authority but God had to remind him to use it. Many times we stand before a mountain and praying for God to move it and God says "speak to it".

Mark 11:22-23 says:

> "Jesus answered and said to them, 'Have faith in God. For assuredly, I say to you, whoever says to this mountain, "Be removed and be cast into the sea," and does not doubt in his heart, but believes that those things he says will be done, he will have whatever he says'."

This is prayer that speaks directly to a situation. With this prayer you address mountains.

Mountains are obstructions to your destiny, your prosperity and your blessings. They could be spoken words, negative things that people have spoken into your life. Or perhaps worry or anxiety. As you move towards accomplishing your destiny, there are going to be things in your way that you need to command to move. I mean the things that say you are a failure, things that say you can't make it, things that say you are useless. Say to those things "Be thou removed, be thou cast into the sea." It is time to go to the next level. Exercise the keys that God has given you.

PROPHETIC PRAYER

Prophetic prayer is when you speak the mind of God into situations. You need to know the mind of God in order to speak it. In prophetic prayers you make decrees and declarations. For example when Jesus was born and was brought into the temple, the Bible says there was a man in the temple who began to make prophetic declarations over Him. So you make prophetic declarations on your children knowing what God has spoken to you about them. Every morning you declare "they will make it, they will fulfill their destiny, there is a task that God has set before them, they will never turn to the left or to the right". Make declarations into their lives. It is not the will of God that any marriage should fail. Make those declarations into your relationship. "This relationship is meant to set a good example, to experience all the romance that God intended." Read the Book of Solomon. Speak it into your marriage.

Luke 11:2 is a prophetic prayer. It says, *"Your kingdom come. Your will be done on earth as it is in heaven"*. Pray the kingdom of God into situations, into cities, into people's lives, into your relationships, into your job, into your country, into the world! Wherever the kingdom of God comes, darkness will be pushed back. Make prophetic declarations.

Psalms 1:3 says:

> "He shall be like a tree planted by the rivers of water, that brings forth its fruit in its season, whose leaf also shall not wither; And whatever he does shall prosper."

Declare that into your life. Say "I will position myself in places where I will prosper. I will be a fruit-bearing Christian." Come against negative things in your life. Pray for right relationships to come into your life. Say "Lord, I speak the right people into my life, who will help me fulfill my destiny".

CONTEMPLATIVE PRAYER

In contemplative prayer you enter into God's silence. You quiet your spirit in order to hear God's voice. Psalms 62:1 says, *"Truly my soul silently waits for God; from Him comes my salvation"*. I am not talking about a "quicky" prayer....one that is thirty seconds. Sometimes it can be an hour where you open your heart and your soul to receive from God.

There are several benefits to contemplative prayer. Let me name just three:

1. *Reflection*

Here you think about God's goodness, His Word and His power. We tend to forget about the doings of God in our lives. So we need to stop once in awhile to see how God has been taking care of us. Contemplative prayer places you in the position where you can remember the doings of God.

2. *Renewal*

Isaiah 40:28-30 says:

> "Have you not known? Have you not heard? The ever-lasting God, the Lord, The Creator of the ends of the earth, neither faints nor is weary. His understanding is unsearchable. He gives power to the weak, and to those who have no might He increases strength. Even the youths shall faint and be weary, and the young men shall utterly fall, but those who wait on the Lord shall renew their strength; They shall mount up with wings like eagles, they shall run and not be weary, they shall walk and not faint."

When we are tired and stressed then let your words be few and wait on the Lord.

3. *Receiving*

Matthew 4:4 says:

> "But He answered and said, 'It is written, "Man shall not live by bread alone, but by every word that proceeds from the mouth of God'."

Contemplative prayer is when I receive from the mouth of the Lord. I always long to receive from the mouth of the Lord. Sometimes He says nothing. But I know that even in His silence He is speaking volumes to me.

CHAPTER FOUR

THE PRAYER LIFE OF JESUS

Many believers today do not have an effective prayer life. We need to learn from the prayerful life of Jesus. A careful reading of the New Testament will show that He has set an example for us to follow.

DEVOTIONAL PRAYER LIFE

Jesus had a routine of getting up regularly in the morning to pray. Mark 1:35 summarizes it this way:

> "Very early in the morning, while it was still dark, Jesus got up, left the house and went off to a solitary place, where he prayed " *(NIV)*.

1. Priority

The first thing we notice about Jesus' devotional prayer is that prayer was a priority to Jesus. Mark 1:35, *"Very early in the morning..."(NIV)*. And it doesn't matter how busy he was. Luke 5:15:

> "Yet the news about him spread all the more, so that

crowds of people came to hear him and to be healed of their sicknesses. But Jesus often withdrew to lonely places and prayed. (*NIV*)

So you see, Jesus was a busy man! Yet He, "…often withdrew…and prayed." Jesus Christ had only three years to accomplish the destiny for which He was born. Yet He made time to withdraw for prayer. You are not too busy to pray. In fact because you are so busy you need to pray. Prayer will sustain you through your busy life.

Because prayer was such a priority, He made sure that He did it first thing in the morning. There are so many distractions in our lives that if we don't do it first thing, it will likely never be done. You may not be a morning person but if you don't get up early to pray it is not going to be done. So this means you set the alarm, get up and go pray. And because you are not a morning person, make sure you go to bed early so that you can wake up feeling refreshed. Staying up to watch a movie or on Facebook till one 1am will not help you much as far as prayer is concern. You have to check your priorities and rearrange your life so that you can meet the living God.

Also go to bed with the Bible or worship music on your mind. You will wake up fresh and ready for the Presence of God. How you go to bed will determine how you wake up. Before the morning began for Jesus He had already done His quiet time. Before anyone is awake, before the kids are getting ready for school, you should be already up praying.

Psalms 63:1 says:

> "O God, You are my God; Early will I seek You; My soul thirsts for You; My flesh longs for You in a dry and thirsty land where there is no water."

Show me any man or woman of God and I will show you a person who makes prayer a priority in their life. Begin tomorrow morning. Some of you ladies are used to getting up at 6:30 a.m. and having a shower and doing your makeup. Now get up at 6 a.m. to pray!

Jesus rose early in the morning to pray because He was passionate about prayer. You will rise up early to do whatever you are passionate about. During the soccer world cup, many of us were waking very early to catch our favorite teams. If you have to do something at 5am you will find a way to get up. If you have an interview for a job, you will find a way to get up. If we are going to get anywhere with Jesus Christ we must be passionate about our relationship with Him and make it our priority. Start your day with Jesus and I can assure you God is going to give you victory.

2. Place

Jesus made prayer a priority, He also had selected places to pray. Mark 1:35 says:

> "Very early in the morning, while it was still dark, Jesus got up, left the house and went off to a solitary place, ..." *(NIV)*

There were different places Jesus would go to pray to minimize distractions. I have my own place to seek God where there is no TV, phone or internet to distract me. There will inevitably be someone calling or texting when you are praying. Go somewhere in your house where technology is not welcome.

Matthew 14:22-23:

> "Immediately Jesus made His disciples get into the boat and go before Him to the other side, while He sent the multitudes away. And when He had sent the multitudes away, He went up on the mountain by Himself to pray. Now when evening came, He was alone there."

That was His base. He was either going to the mountain or the wilderness; His solitary place. Somewhere very quiet where no one would disturb Him. Why? Because if God is going to talk to you, if He is going to get your attention, you need to get rid of the distractions. You can't make it in this life without the voice of God. Jesus said:

> "Man shall not live by bread alone, but by every word that proceeds from the mouth of God." *(Matthew 4:4)*

There are words proceeding out of God's mouth that we cannot hear unless we wait on Him. We need to find the time to go and meet Him at our particular place.

Daniel 6:10 says:

> "Now when Daniel knew that the writing was signed, he went home. And in his upper room, with his windows

open toward Jerusalem, he knelt down on his knees three times that day, and prayed and gave thanks before his God, as was his custom since early days."

Daniel had his "place." It was his upper room. Some of you may have only one bedroom, and you and your children are all crammed in there. But you can still find a place. It may be the washroom! When we first came to North America, all we could afford was a one bedroom basement with one tiny washroom. The door to the washroom was a closet door. My daughter was about three years old at that time and she knew that Daddy goes into the washroom to pray. It was my holy place. That is where God spoke to me. It doesn't matter where your "place" is. Even if it is in the belly of the fish in the bottom of the ocean, God will speak to you.

Matthew 6:6 also says:

> "But thou, when thou prayest, enter into thy closet, and when thou hast shut thy door, pray to thy Father which is in secret; and thy Father which seeth in secret shall reward thee openly." *(KJV)*

In today's culture we are busy with everything except the closet. But that is where we need to be! We wonder why we are so anxious, so depressed, so afraid, so burnt out, always on the edge, and always angry? We are not meeting Him in the closet. If your house has a coat closet then you have a prayer room. There is a brother I know who does that. He has taken out all his coats from his closet and turned it into a place of prayer. When He goes in there, God knows that His son is ready to meet with Him. Find your place and let your heavenly Father meet you there.

3. Practice

Jesus made prayer His priority. He went to His place. And there he prayed! He practiced prayer on a regular basis. When we repeat an activity regularly our effectiveness in that activity improves. Just as athletes train for competitive events we must train for the race God has called us to run. As we practice our prayers we become more effective in them. We will discuss in detail how to practice prayer in the next chapter.

PROLONGED PRAYER LIFE

Apart from His devotional life, Jesus' life was marked by times of prolonged prayer. Having a regular time to meet with God is just the starting point. We also need extensive times of prayer with God. Luke 6:12 says:

> "Now it came to pass in those days that He went out to the mountain to pray, and continued all night in prayer to God."

Some people have queried why we pray all-night at church. My answer always is "Why not"? Jesus prayed all-night. And His prayer life is an example for us to follow. There are times when you need to travail long in prayer until you receive an answer.

Jesus prayed all night in order to choose the right leaders. The Bible says the next morning He called His followers to Him and chose twelve disciples. Do you remember the last time a church board prayed all-night to choose a pastor? Instead we have our list of qualifications. They check which school you went to; how many sermons you have preached and the size of your last church. And then they negotiate your salary and benefits.

In 2 Corinthians 6:4-5, Paul says:

> "But in all things approving ourselves as the ministers of God, in much patience, in afflictions, in necessities, in distresses, In stripes, in imprisonments, in tumults, in labours, in watchings, in fastings." *(KJV)*

This is Paul's resume and I love it! "Watchings", that is all-night prayer. Paul says "I do this often." He also fasted regularly. We will explore the practice of fasting more deeply in chapter seven. There are times in your life where you need to have prolonged times of prayer. When do we need to do a prolonged prayer?

First, when we need to make some important decisions. There are some life changing choices that can be costly if we make the wrong decisions. Seek the face of God when you are looking for a marriage partner. Don't just say "God, if you want me to marry then let the woman come to my house, Amen." That is foolishness. I know a man in his prime who prayed like that. He said "Lord I am ready to marry so the first woman who knocks on my door wearing a red dress let her be the woman I am to marry." And in less than thirty seconds he was done. Few hours later somebody knocks on the door and she was wearing red but she was 80 years old! As soon as he saw the woman he cried out to the Lord, "Oh Lord, no, no, have mercy".

Take time to pray when you need to make an important decision. You may have to spend the whole day in prayer or all -night in prayer. Proverbs 3: 5-6 says:

> "Trust in the Lord with all your heart, And lean not on your own understanding; In all your ways acknowledge Him, and He shall direct your paths."

Second, we do prolonged prayer when we need special empowerment to do God's work. Jesus started His ministry with forty days of prayer and fasting. The Bible says He returned from the wilderness in the power of the Spirit. If we are going to do God's work in God's way, then we need to wait upon Him for special empowerment.

Lastly, we do prolonged prayers when we need breakthroughs. Sometimes you come to a place in your life where certain mountains need to be moved, and you are running out of time. You need answers, not tomorrow, but right now! Jacob was a man like that. He wrestled with an angel all-night until he got his breakthrough.

PASSIONATE PRAYER LIFE

Something else we notice about Jesus' prayer life was that

His prayers were real. He prayed from the heart, not in religious jargon. I have noticed some believers have special accents and vocabulary when they pray. I mean the African brother who prays in an American accent and uses words that he normally does not use in everyday conversation. That's how the Pharisees use to pray. Luke 18:9-14 says:

> "Also He spoke this parable to some who trusted in themselves that they were righteous, and despised others: 'Two men went up to the temple to pray, one a Pharisee and the other a tax collector. The Pharisee stood and prayed thus with himself, "God, I thank You that I am not like other men—extortioners, unjust, adulterers, or even as this tax collector. I fast twice a week; I give tithes of all that I possess." And the tax collector, standing afar off, would not so much as raise his eyes to heaven, but beat his breast, saying, 'God, be merciful to me a sinner!' I tell you, this man went down to his house justified rather than the other; for everyone who exalts himself will be humbled, and he who humbles himself will be exalted."

The tax collector was not going through a religious duty. Rather the Bible says he was "beating his chest." Jesus affirmed his prayer. A prayer from the heart! Prayer that is real.

Concerning Jesus' prayers, Hebrews 5:7 says:

> "While Jesus was here on earth, he offered prayers and pleadings, with a loud cry and tears, to the one who could rescue him from death. And God heard his prayers because of his deep reverence for God." (*NLT*)

He prayed with loud cries and tears. What makes you cry? When was the last time you cried in prayer? Does the presence of God make you cry? Over and over again the book of Psalms tells us to cry out to the Lord. Show some real emotions. There are some people who pray in such a dull manner that they can put you off prayer; it's boring! There is no heart. Psalm 61:1-3 says:

> "Hear my cry, O God; attend to my prayer. From the end of the earth I will cry to You, When my heart is overwhelmed; Lead me to the rock that is higher than I. For You have been a shelter for me, A strong tower from the enemy."

David was a man's man and soldier's soldier. And yet, he often cried to God in prayer. Real men cry in prayer. David fought when he was on the battlefield, and he also cried in God's presence. No wonder the Bible calls him "a man after God's own heart." Open your heart and pour out to God. Tell God how you really, really feel.

Carly Fiorina, was the former CEO of the multinational technology company Hewlett Packard. She was once asked by an interviewer what she regretted most at her time with HP. To which she responded, "I regret crying before the board members who fired me. They did not deserve my tears." Your ex-wife or husband does not deserve your tears. Nobody deserves your tears. In fact don't show your enemy your tears. Show your tears to God, for He deserves it and He will help you through! The Bible says of Hannah, "and she was in bitterness of soul, and prayed to the LORD and wept in anguish." She refused to show her tears to her enemy. Rather she cried out unto her God!

PERSISTENT PRAYER LIFE

We also notice in the prayer life of Jesus that He prayed over and over again on the same subject. Somebody said to me once that praying again on the same subject shows a lack of faith. To the contrary, in most cases it shows our trust in the living God. Mathew 26:39-44 says:

> "He went a little farther and fell on His face, and prayed, saying, 'O My Father, if it is possible, let this cup pass from Me; nevertheless, not as I will, but as You will."….Again, a second time, He went away and prayed, saying, 'O My Father, if this cup cannot pass away from Me unless I drink it, Your will be done.' …So He left them, went away again, and prayed the third time, saying the same words."

So you see, there is nothing wrong in coming back to God with the same request. It is called persistent prayer, as described in the previous chapter.

In Luke chapter two, the Bible describes a prophetess called Anna. She was very old and her husband had died. And instead of waiting and worrying about her next husband, she went to the temple and stayed there day and night praying for the coming Messiah. She prayed on the same thing over and over until God answered her prayer and Jesus was brought into the temple. Persistent prayer never gives up!

PRAYER OF AGREEMENT

The final aspect of the prayer life of Jesus was that He prayed with others. Luke 9:28:

> "About eight days later Jesus took Peter, John, and James up on a mountain to pray." *(NLT)*

There are times when you need people to pray alongside you. Praying all the time by yourself is not as powerful as praying with others. I will deal with this in detail in the chapter "The Power of United Prayer."

Take advantage of all the prayer meetings in your church, and if there are none, start one. Find personal prayer partners. Peter, James and John were Jesus' personal prayer partners. Find yours!

Our Savior Jesus Christ has set an example of prayer for us to follow. Let's follow it.

CHAPTER FIVE

JESUS TAUGHT US HOW TO PRAY

The Bible says in Luke 11:1:

> "Now it came to pass, as He was praying in a certain place, when He ceased, that one of His disciples said to Him, "Lord, teach us to pray, as John also taught his disciples."

The disciples saw Jesus preach, but never asked Him to teach them how to preach. They saw Him witness with the power of the Holy Spirit, but never asked Him to teach them how to witness. They could have asked Jesus to help them make some money because they were broke. No, they simply asked Him to teach them how to pray. So He began to teach what has become popularly known as "The Lord's Prayer." In this prayer, He lays out a blueprint of how to bang on the doors of heaven. In other words, this is how you need to pray if you want your prayer to be heard or to receive a breakthrough...or to change your destiny.

This prayer is a very short prayer. In fact it is one of the shortest prayers in the Bible, consisting of only sixty-six words. Yet it the most popular prayer of all time. So how do we pray like Jesus? Luke 11:2-4 says:

> "He said to them, 'When you pray, say: Our Father in heaven, Hallowed be Your name. Your kingdom come. Your will be done on earth as it is in heaven. Give us day by day our daily bread. And forgive us our sins, for we also forgive everyone who is indebted to us. And do not lead us into temptation, but deliver us from the evil one'."

PRAYER OF PRAISE

Jesus says we must begin our prayer with praise. Luke 11:2 says, *"Our Father in heaven, Hallowed (holy) be Your name"*. Declaring God's holiness is the highest praise we can give Him. When you say to God "Hallowed be your name" you are giving Him the highest praise. The angels in heaven do not say "Majesty, majesty, majesty," although God is full of majesty. They do not say "Gracious, gracious, gracious," although God is gracious. Day and night before the throne they cry *"Holy, Holy, Holy unto the Lord" (Revelation 4:8)*.

The Bible says, *"Worship the Lord in the beauty of His holiness" (Psalms 96:9)*. Holiness is who God is. It is one of the things that separates God from us. When Isaiah saw the Cherubim and the Seraphim before the throne, they were also saying, *"Holy, Holy, Holy unto the Lord" (Isaiah 6:3)*.

When we praise God, we are expressing our ultimate purpose. Contrary to popular belief, our primary purpose on earth is not to make money and be happy. Our primary purpose is to glorify God. That is why the first thing out of your mouth every morning should be "God, I bless you." The Psalmist says:

> "I will bless the Lord at all times, His praise shall be continually in my mouth." *(Psalms 34:1)*

Why? Because that is why we are here. We are created to worship.

Praise unlocks the heart of God. Just as there are keys a young man can use to unlock the heart of a woman, praise is one of the keys that unlocks the heart of God. Psalm 100:4 says:

> "Enter into His gates with thanksgiving, and into His courts with praise. Be thankful to Him, and bless His name."

Come before Him, not with prayer requests; come before Him not with burdens. Come before Him with singing! Praise brings you in to the throne room.

Praise creates breakthroughs. Acts 16:24-25 says:

> "Having received such a charge, he put them into the inner prison and fastened their feet in the stocks. But at midnight Paul and Silas were praying and singing hymns to God, and the prisoners were listening to them."

That's what you do when you feel overwhelmed. That's what you do when you feel bound. That's what you do when you've just received bad news. That's what you do when you have come to the end of your line and feeling like giving up.

Why? Because that brings the power and the presence of God into your situation. Paul knew that. I can imagine Paul saying to Silas, "Hey Silas are you alright? I know you are in chains but can we praise God? We may not be able to dance but we can sing hymns." And Silas responding, "I'm in". Paul may not have been able to carry a tune but it does not matter. It is the heart that counts.

The Bible says:

> "Suddenly there was a great earthquake, so that the foundations of the prison were shaken; and immediately all the doors were opened and everyone's chains were loosed." *(Acts 16:26)*

Can you imagine? An earthquake because two men were singing! I believe the earthquake was God saying "I am coming through for you". Those of you who think there is no power in singing need to change your theology. There is power in singing. It breaks my heart to see people sing in church like they are just going through a routine. The power of praise has the capability to change your soul and situation.

They did not ask God to loosen their chains. They did not ask God to set them free. They simply praised God! Remember my friend, as you praise God He is healing your diseases; as you praise God He is delivering you from your depression; and as you praise God He is touching all your loved ones. Praise Him at all times!

PRAYER OF PURPOSE

Jesus also taught His disciples to say, *"Your kingdom come…"(Luke 11:2)*. Quite often when we come before God, we are anxious to talk to God about our problems. But before we do so, we need to first focus on God's kingdom. In fact Jesus says that we should:

> "… seek first the kingdom of God and His righteousness, and all these things shall be added to you."
> *(Matthew 6:33)*

When you take care of God's business, He will take care of your business. Because we are selfish by nature, we tend to focus mostly on ourselves. Even when we are looking for a church to join, we look for what is in it for us. Instead we should say, "God how can I serve your kingdom in this church?" Remember, life is not about us. It is about God and His kingdom. When we say "Your kingdom come," what we are saying is "Lord I lay my dreams, my ambitions, my burdens, my visions, and every plan of mine at Your feet". God answers these kinds of prayers.

"Your kingdom come" is a submissive prayer. You are recognizing Jesus as your King. A kingdom is where a king rules. Jesus is Savior and King. The two titles are equally important, but they are different. Jesus can be your Savior and not your King. As your Savior He saved you, He died for you, He forgave your past, present and future sins, and He set you free. But as your King you have to surrender your will to Him. When you say "Your Kingdom come" you are

saying "Jesus You are the King of my life, when you speak I obey.

"Your kingdom come" is an evangelistic prayer. What you are saying is for God's Kingdom to increase. To increase in your community. To increase in your city. To increase in your country and to increase on all the continents. You are praying for God's rule in the hearts of men and women to increase. You are praying for God to change the hearts of sinners and bring home the backsliders.

"Your kingdom come" is also a warfare prayer. It is a prayer to cause the kingdom of darkness to fall. Jesus said:

> "If I by the finger of God cast out devils then the Kingdom of God has come to you." *(Matthew 12:28)*

The kingdom of God comes when we destroy the kingdom of darkness. We cannot build God's kingdom on top of the kingdom of darkness. The Bible says Satan is the god of this world *(2 Corinthians 4:-3-4)*. So we need to uproot him in order to establish God's kingdom. According to Jesus, you cannot go to a strongman's house and take his goods without first binding the strongman *(Matthew 12:29)*. So when we say "Your kingdom come" we are stepping into a war zone. We are declaring "devil, your kingdom will not stand!"

Jesus says:

> "... I will build My church, and the gates of Hades shall not prevail against it." *(Mathew 16:18)*

"Your kingdom come" is also a protest prayer. This prayer rejects any other man-made kingdom in society. It rejects the kingdom of materialism. It rejects the kingdom of humanism. It rejects any philosophy of men and it rejects the kingdom of intellectualism. It is declaring loud and clear, "Lord let Your kingdom reign, and let all human kingdoms fall.

And finally, *"Your kingdom come" is a prophetic prayer.* We are praying for Jesus to come quickly and establish His final rule over all the world. You are declaring that, "This world is not my home". You are reminding yourself that you are only here for a short time. Sometimes we forget and we live like we are going be here forever. It's in the next life that we are going to live forever. The devil likes to keep our focus on the here and now. I challenge you to pray "Your kingdom come…" and keep your eyes up. As Colossians 3:1-2 says:

> "If then you were raised with Christ, seek those things which are above, where Christ is, sitting at the right hand of God. Set your mind on things above, not on things on the earth."

Anytime you are going through a tough situation, keep your eyes up! Put everything in eternal perspective. I preach every Sunday like tomorrow I will not be alive. I give everything I've got. There is no guarantee how long I will live. All of us have an expiry date on our lives. We don't know the date our lives will expire. "Thy Kingdom come", we could go home any moment.

PRAYER FOR PROVISION

Jesus also taught His disciples to pray, *"Give us this day our daily bread" (Luke 11:3).* This is where you bring your personal requests to God. This prayer recognizes God as your source. Sometimes we think we, by our own strength, provide for our needs. Imagine if God takes your breath away from you. You will be dead! We owe our very lives to God. You sleep and wake up without realizing who is keeping you alive. Some people slept and did not wake this morning. Others woke up and did not have any feelings in their legs. They may never walk again. "Give us this day our daily bread" recognizes God as the source of all our blessings. Deuteronomy 8:14-18 says:

> "When your heart is lifted up, and you forget the Lord your God who brought you out of the land of Egypt, from the house of bondage; who led you through that great and terrible wilderness, in which were fiery serpents and scorpions and thirsty land where there was no water; who brought water for you out of the flinty rock; who fed you in the wilderness with manna, which your fathers did not know, that He might humble you and that He might test you, to do you good in the end— then you say in your heart, 'My power and the might of my hand have gained me this wealth.' And you shall remember the Lord your God, for it is He who gives you power to get wealth, that He may establish His covenant which He swore to your fathers, as it is this day."

May we never come to that place. When was the last time

you actually stopped to thank God for your food? I am including your Starbucks coffee. What about a cup of water? There are many families around the world who live without safe drinking water. Give thanks for all He has blessed you with.

This prayer also recognizes God as your supplier. As Philippians 4:19 says:

> "And my God shall supply all your need according to His riches in glory by Christ Jesus."

PRAYER FOR PARDON

Jesus taught us to pray:

> "And forgive us our sins, for we also forgive everyone who is indebted to us." *(Luke 11:4)*

This is a prayer for cleansing and washing. Why is the prayer of pardon so important? In Isaiah 59:1-2 we read:

> "Behold, the Lord's hand is not shortened, that it cannot save; Nor His ear heavy, that it cannot hear. But your iniquities have separated you from your God; And your sins have hidden His face from you, so that He will not hear."

Sin blocks our blessings. Confession of sins has to be like breathing. You breathe in oxygen, but breathe out the toxic carbon dioxide. Sin is like a toxin that you need to let out of your system otherwise it will destroy you. If you sense sin in your life, confess it immediately.

Sin breaks fellowship with God. Isaiah says:

> "your iniquities have separated you from God."
> (*Isaiah 59:2*)

Sin also breaches our security. Sin gives the devil an entrance into our lives. Ephesians 4:26-27:

> "'Be angry, and do not sin': do not let the sun go down on your wrath, nor give place to the devil."

When you go to sleep angry, the Bible says you are opening the door for the devil. God protects us but sin breaks that security and allows the enemy to come in. The enemy can only do work in your life if you are not in right standing with God.

PRAYER FOR PROTECTION

Jesus taught us to pray, *"And do not lead us into temptation, But deliver us from the evil one" (Luke 11:4).* This is a warfare zone. Warfare is part of our prayer. God is good and He loves us. The devil also is real and he hates us. Jesus says:

> "The thief comes not but to steal, to kill, and to destroy." (*John 10:10, KJV*)

We are under constant attack. Psalms 91: 5-6 says:

> "You shall not be afraid of the terror by night, nor of the arrow that flies by day, nor of the pestilence that walks in darkness, nor of the destruction that lays waste at noonday."

The day you declared yourself as a child of God, you became fair game. 1 Peter 5:8-9 says:

> "Be sober, be vigilant; because your adversary the devil walks about like a roaring lion, seeking whom he may devour. Resist him, steadfast in the faith, knowing that the same sufferings are experienced by your brotherhood in the world."

That is why we need to pray "God! Lead us not into temptation, deliver us from the evil one." We need God's protection! There are three ways God protects us:

1. *Army of Angels*

Whether you see them or not you are surrounded by hosts of angels. We are not alone, we are protected and the enemy cannot penetrate. 2 Kings 6:15-17:

> "And when the servant of the man of God arose early and went out, there was an army, surrounding the city with horses and chariots. And his servant said to him, 'Alas, my master! What shall we do?' So he answered, "Do not fear, for those who are with us are more than those who are with them." And Elisha prayed, and said, 'Lord, I pray, open his eyes that he may see.' Then the Lord opened the eyes of the young man, and he saw. And behold, the mountain was full of horses and chariots of fire all around Elisha."

Elijah was calm while his servant was anxious because he could not see the protection. I pray that God will open your eyes to see what Elijah saw.

We are all surrounded by angels. It is why the devil couldn't touch Job. The enemy wanted to attack but he couldn't. Why? *"For You have made a hedge around him and around his household" (Job 1:10).* Your protection extends to your wife, your children and your property. God protects your family and your property. The Bible says:

> "As the mountains surround Jerusalem, so the Lord surrounds His people from this time forth and forever." *(Psalm 125:2)*

We have an army of angels on guard for us.

2. Blood of the Lamb

Exodus 12:23 says:

> "For the Lord will pass through to strike the Egyptians; and when He sees the blood on the lintel and on the two doorposts, the Lord will pass over the door and not allow the destroyer to come into your houses to strike you."

1 Corinthians 7:5 says:

> "Therefore purge out the old leaven, that you may be a new lump, since you truly are unleavened. For indeed Christ, our Passover, was sacrificed for us."

You are covered and the devil must pass over because of the redemptive power of Jesus. Revelation 12:11 says:

> "And they overcame him by the blood of the Lamb and by the word of their testimony, and they did not love their lives to the death."

3. *Armor of God*

We are protected by the armor of God. Now God does the first two on our behalf, but this one you must do yourself. Ephesians 6:10-11:

> "Finally, my brethren, be strong in the Lord and in the power of His might. Put on the whole armor of God, that you may be able to stand against the wiles of the devil."

Protect your mind by putting on "the helmet of Salvation." Protect it against anxiety, temptation, and depression. Some of us cannot sleep at night because we are burdened with worry. We must put on the helmet of Salvation!

You protect your heart by putting on "the breastplate of righteousness." There is an ongoing battle for your heart. Keep your heart pure. There are things in the world that are ready to mess up your heart every time you step out. Jesus says:

> "So the scribe said to Him, 'Well said, Teacher. You have spoken the truth, for there is one God, and there is no other but He. And to love Him with all the heart, with all the understanding, with all the soul, and with all the strength, and to love one's neighbor as oneself, is more than all the whole burnt offerings and sacrifices."
> (*Mark 12:32-33*)

Protect your heart and its passions. The world wants you to love temporal things. As 1 John 2:15-17 warns, "Do not love the world or the things in the world. If anyone loves the world, the love of the Father is not in him. For all that is in the world—the lust of the flesh, the lust of the eyes, and the pride of life—is not of the Father but is of the world. And the world is passing away, and the lust of it; but he who does the will of God abides forever". Let's love Jesus. It is how we are most fulfilled. This is how Jesus taught us to pray.

CHAPTER SIX

THE POWER OF UNITED PRAYER

In Mark 11:17 Jesus said:

> "My house shall be called a house of prayer for all nations."

He expects prayer to be a top priority of His people when they gather. And we understand from the reading of Book of Acts that the Apostles made prayer a priority. They gave themselves continually in prayer *(Acts 6:4)*. Today we seem to gather for everything except prayer. Jesus did not say "My house shall be a house of preaching", although preaching is important. Someone once said that Sunday morning attendance shows the popularity of the preacher, but attendance to the prayer meetings shows the popularity of Christ. When I meet pastors who tell me they have a church of a thousand or five thousand people, I usually ask them about the prayer meetings attendance. Those are the real members. The church that is not praying is playing.

What the church needs most today is more prayer not more books. Do you know that there are more books written about marriage in our generation than any other generation? And yet our divorce rate has never been higher. It's not because of lack of knowledge. What marriages need is prayer! What we need today is not more family experts. Prayer is what is going to bring our prodigal children back home. Prayer is what is going to bring your wayward husband home. Prayer is what is going to shift your difficult situation. Prayer will move your mountain. Stop focusing on buying books and get on your knees. There is power in prayers.

Gradually churches are replacing godly counsellors with professional counsellors. I am not against them but they are not what the church needs. What we need are counsellors who know how to seek the face of God, counsellors who are sensitive to the Holy Spirit, counsellors who know how to heal the sick. Jesus is the answer to our brokenness. He came to bind our broken hearts.

We have taken prayer out of the church and replaced it with secular methods. Jeremiah was addressing exactly this when he said, "For My people have committed two evils: They have forsaken Me, the fountain of living waters, and hewn themselves cisterns—broken cisterns that can hold no water".

Everything we do, say, or accomplish must be birthed in prayer. I heard a story about a Korean missionary who came to America. He said he was amazed what the church in America was able to accomplish without prayer. Sometimes I wonder if we are building the church of Christ or creating an organization or spiritual country clubs. The church was birthed in prayer *(Acts 2)*. That which is birthed in prayer can only be sustained in prayer. Is it any wonder that the church has become so powerless? Prayerlessness leads to powerlessness. Today we can no longer cast out demons. We can no longer heal the sick and perform signs and wonders like the Apostles did.

Until the church returns to praying, it is better she close her doors and put up a sign saying, "Not open for business". At Calvary Worship Center, we are open for business: the Master's business, and the most important thing that will strike you when you come to Calvary Worship Center is not the preaching or the people, although there is good preaching and the people are wonderful, comprising of over eighty nations. Rather it is the prayers. There is a prayer meeting in the building EVERYDAY. And there is prayer going 24/7 in homes. Everything we do is birthed and bathed in prayer. Without Him we can do nothing.

I believe one of the reasons churches don't gather to pray is because we don't know the power of united prayer. Let me outline a few.

First, when we unite in prayer we attract *God's Presence.* We know God is everywhere. It is called the omnipresence. But there are moments when God visibly manifests Himself. Jesus says in John 14:23:

> "He who has My commandments and keeps them, it is he who loves Me. And he who loves Me will be loved by

My Father, and I will love him and manifest Myself to
him."

In other words there are certain gatherings that attract
God's presence. In Acts 4, we are told that Peter and John
were threatened by the authorities and freed. And as soon as
they were freed they didn't go home to have a barbeque.
No! Rather they went straight to a prayer meeting, where:

> "And when they had prayed, the place where they were
> assembled together was shaken; and they were all filled
> with the Holy Spirit, and they spoke the word of God
> with boldness." *(verse 31)*

Their prayers attracted the presence of God. And God visited them in a style. In an earthquake. The Bible also says
when Paul and Silas prayed there was an earthquake,

I have done a little research on the connection between the
presence of God and the earthquakes in the Book of Acts. I
believe the answer is in Revelation 8:3-5:

> "Then another angel, having a golden censer, came and
> stood at the altar. He was given much incense, that he
> should offer it with the prayers of all the saints upon the
> golden altar which was before the throne. And the
> smoke of the incense, with the prayers of the saints, as-
> cended before God from the angel's hand. Then the an-
> gel took the censer, filled it with fire from the altar, and
> threw it to the earth. And there were noises, thunderings,
> lightnings, and an earthquake."

Do you see that? When the people of God pray, the angels

take our prayers and mix it with incense. They then release our prayers back on earth. The results are earthquake, thunder and flashes of lightning! That's what our prayers can do. The angels in heaven are waiting! They are waiting to mix our prayers with the incense. Is yours in?

Sometimes God manifests His presence in the form of smoke *(see Isaiah 6)*. It is very sad today to see churches create their own smoke through smoke (fog) machines. Because we can't attract the real thing we have created substitutes. That's idolatry. And may God help us.

Second, when we unite in prayer we release **God's Power.** Prayer connects you to the power source. It doesn't matter how expensive or powerful your electronic device is, it is useless if not connected to a power outlet. Our church building or people may be beautiful but if we are not connected to God, we are useless to the world.

One of my professors in seminary said to us once that the days of signs and wonders have passed. To which I responded, "God has not stopped working miracles and signs. The problem is that the church is not connected to the power outlet." Show me a praying church and I will show you a powerful church. There is a release of power upon the people of God, when they pray.

One day I had a problem with my microwave. And I tried everything to get it to work with results. Then I finally I called an electrician friend of mine. He said to me, after inspecting the machine, "Pastor, do you know your machine is unplugged?" He made me looked really stupid. But unfortunately, the same is true of the church today. We are trying to do God's work without any connection to Him, and we are wondering why we don't have the results the Apostles had. We need to go back to the power source. Jesus says in John 14:12:

> "Most assuredly, I say to you, he who believes in Me, the works that I do he will do also; and greater works than these he will do, because I go to My Father."

We cannot do greater works until we start praying like Jesus. Are we willing to pay the price? Luke 4:14 says:

> "Then Jesus returned in the power of the Spirit to Galilee..."

What did He return from? 40 days of fasting and prayer in the wilderness! Oh, He was charged!

Let me show you what power can do.

- ***First, power will help the church to preach the Gospel.***

Acts 1:8 says:

> "But you shall receive power when the Holy Spirit has come upon you; and you shall be witnesses to Me in Jerusalem, and in all Judea and Samaria, and to the end of the earth."

Preaching under the power of the Holy Spirit is the preaching that transforms lives. Acts 2:37-38:

Now when they heard this, they were cut to the heart, and said to Peter and the rest of the apostles, "Men and brethren, what shall we do?" Then Peter said to them, "Repent, and let every one of you be baptized in the name of Jesus Christ for the remission of sins; and you shall receive the gift of the Holy Spirit."

What is happening to preaching these days? We apologize when people feel convicted. Peter said "Repent!" When the power of the Holy Spirit comes upon you, you can't preach whatever you like. You preach what God wants you to preach, and the true Gospel brings conviction. These days, people want to become Christians without first repenting. They want to become Christians without giving up anything. Some preaching, unfortunately, just makes us feel good.

When Stephen was full of the Holy Spirit and he preached, exactly the same day, the Bible says the listeners were cut to the heart, to the point that they stoned him to death *(Acts 7:54-60)*. That's the Gospel. The Gospel that does not call us into repentance is another gospel. John the Baptist came preaching saying:

"Repent for the Kingdom of God is at hand."
(Matthew 3:2).

When the prodigal son came home he said,

"Father, I have sinned against heaven and in your sight, and am no longer worthy to be called your son."
(Luke 15:21)

- ### *Second, power will let the church perform miracles.*

Acts 3:6-8 says:

> "Then Peter said, 'Silver and gold I do not have, but what
> I do have I give you: In the name of Jesus Christ of Naza-
> reth, rise up and walk.' And he took him by the right
> hand and lifted him up, and immediately his feet and an-
> kle bones received strength. So he, leaping up, stood and
> walked and entered the temple with them—walking,
> leaping, and praising God."

These men were on their way to a prayer meeting. They
were broke but they had power. I'd rather be broke and perform miracles than be rich and powerless. Unfortunately
that's the story of most churches in the West. The church in
Laodicea was like that. Revelation 3:15-19 says:

> "I know your works, that you are neither cold nor hot. I
> could wish you were cold or hot. So then, because you
> are lukewarm, and neither cold nor hot, I will vomit you
> out of My mouth. Because you say, 'I am rich, have be-
> come wealthy, and have need of nothing'—and do not
> know that you are wretched, miserable, poor, blind, and
> naked—I counsel you to buy from Me gold refined in
> the fire, that you may be rich; and white garments, that
> you may be clothed, that the shame of your nakedness
> may not be revealed; and anoint your eyes with eye salve,
> that you may see. As many as I love, I rebuke and chas-
> ten. Therefore be zealous and repent."

Take away my money, the church buildings and my cars,
but please leave me with the power of the Holy Ghost. Look

at what God is doing in the churches in China, Latin America, Africa, and the rest of the world. They don't have money but they have power! Back in Africa I was broke, but God used me to raise the dead. I saw the crippled walk!

Acts 4:13:

> "Now when they saw the boldness of Peter and John, and perceived that they were uneducated and untrained men, they marveled. And they realized that they had been with Jesus."

You may be foolish and unschooled but people will know you have been with Jesus if you move in the power of the Holy Spirit. Signs and wonders will follow you. The church needs to get back on her knees and see what God is going to do. We are like an army in a valley of dry bones until God breathes His fresh power on us *(Ezekiel 37)*. Are willing to pay the price of prayer?

- **Third, power will help the church to paralyze the Devil.**
  Ephesians 6:10-12 says:

  > "Finally, my brethren, be strong in the Lord and in the power of His might. Put on the whole armor of God, that you may be able to stand against the wiles of the devil. For we do not wrestle against flesh and blood, but against principalities, against powers, against the rulers of the darkness of this age, against spiritual hosts of wickedness in the heavenly places."

Exercising God's power is how we dismantle the works of

darkness. Power will paralyze the enemy. Acts 10:38:

> "how God anointed Jesus of Nazareth with the Holy
> Spirit and with power, who went about doing good and
> healing all who were oppressed by the devil, for God was
> with Him."

Power will release people from bondage. Many people are bound by the devil. I don't want to be part of that Christianity that does not have power to set people free. 2 Timothy 3:5 says:

> "having a form of godliness but denying its power. And
> from such people turn away!"

But our God is mighty to save. He is mighty to deliver. There is nothing the devil fears more than a praying church. When we pray we shake the doors of hell. The ministry of the Apostles was so full of power because they prayed. They healed the sick and cast out demons. Countless number of people surrendered their lives to Christ. Today, I cannot begin to tell you all the gimmicks churches are using to get unbelievers through its doors. They may come in but there will be no true transformation. We need to get back to prayer and leave the rest to God. As we pray, God will attract the people. As we pray God will convict people. We have witnessed this in our church. People being literally drawn into the sanctuary as they walk pass it. People weeping as the preaching is going on.

- **Fourth, power will help the church to activate God's possibilities.**

The Bible says:

> "For with God nothing shall be impossible." *(Luke 1:37)*

And 2 Chronicles 7:14:

> "If My people who are called by My name will humble themselves, and pray and seek My face, and turn from their wicked ways, then I will hear from heaven, and will forgive their sin and heal their land."

Prayer gives us open heavens.

James 4:2 says, *"...you do not have because you do not ask"*. When James was arrested and beheaded, the Bible says the authorities then arrested Peter. And that's where the church drew the line. Acts 12:5:

> "Peter was therefore kept in prison, but constant prayer was offered to God for him by the church."

There comes a time in your life when you have to declare, "Enough is enough! I am sick and tired of the devil kicking me like a soccer ball. I'm sick and tired of the devil ruining my family!" Get on your knees and begin to pray and claim the soul of your child.

Stop whining and start praying. Philippians 4:6-7 says:

> "Be anxious for nothing, but in everything by prayer and supplication, with thanksgiving, let your requests be made known to God; and the peace of God, which surpasses all understanding, will guard your hearts and minds through Christ Jesus."

If God delivered Daniel; if He touched Hannah; and if He healed the blind man; then He will come through for you too!

- ***Finally, power will help us discover God's Plans.***

> "For I know the plans I have for you,' declares the Lord, 'plans to prosper you and not to harm you, plans to give you hope and a future." (*Jeremiah 29:11, NIV*)

God wants to show us His will. Prayer positions us to know it. Prayer makes our spirit sensitive to His voice. The Bible says "He who has an ear, let him hear what the Spirit says to the churches." He is speaking. Are we hearing? Acts 13:1-2 says:

> "Now in the church that was at Antioch there were certain prophets and teachers: Barnabas, Simeon who was called Niger, Lucius of Cyrene, Manaen who had been brought up with Herod the tetrarch, and Saul. As they ministered to the Lord and fasted, the Holy Spirit said, "Now separate to Me Barnabas and Saul for the work to which I have called them."

This was a prayer meeting, and all the leaders were there. Isn't it interesting that today church leaders tell us that prayer is important but they themselves do not attend prayer meetings? Leaders need to lead by example as they did in the Book of Acts.

The Bible says as these leaders "... *ministered to the Lord and fasted...*" (*Acts 13:2*). I like that. Take note of the word "ministered". This means they were praying and worshiping without any particular agenda. Some people call it "soaking prayer". When we "minister" to the Lord, we are simply creating an atmosphere for God to step in. It was in this atmosphere that God said, *"Separate me Paul and Barnabas" (Acts 13:2).*

God will speak to us, when we seek Him. He says in Jeremiah 33:3:

> "Call to Me, and I will answer you, and show you great and mighty things, which you do not know."

God has marvelous plans for us! The condition is to call upon Him. As children of God, we should not struggle to find direction for our lives. He wants to lead us to the "green pastures". He wants to lead you by the "still waters". Let's seek His face.

CHAPTER SEVEN

FASTING AND PRAYER

Fasting and praying is a more intense form of praying. Fasting has always been part of the prayer life of people of God. The Old and New Testaments are full of men and women who fasted and prayed. Moses, Elijah, Ezekiel, Daniel, and the apostles all fasted. Matthew 4:2 says in reference to Jesus, *"After fasting forty days and forty nights, he was hungry".*

The early church fathers also fasted and prayed. Martin Luther was criticized because he fasted too much. John Calvin fasted and prayed until most of Geneva turned to God. John Knox fasted and prayed and the wicked Queen Mary said she feared no weapon like she feared John Knox's prayers. Jonathan Edwards, who was God's instrument in the revival in New England, fasted and prayed. John Wesley fasted twice a week. Charles Finney, one of the greatest spiritual leaders in history, was a man who fasted and prayed. D L Moody was familiar with fasting and praying.

Fasting is becoming a lost discipline in the church today. Like fuel that runs an automotive engine, fasting fuels the prayer life of the people of God. We need to return to it.

THE PRINCIPLES OF FASTING

Fasting is a deliberate and sustained abstinence from all food for a specific period of time *(Ezra 10:6, Esther 4:6, Jonah 2:7)*. The Old Testament word for fast means "covering the mouth," and in the New Testament it means "not to eat". Drinking of water is recommended, especially during prolonged days of fasting. It is said that a person can live without food for forty days, but only three days without water. And in 1 Corinthians 7:5, Paul admonishes married couples to abstain from sex during fasting.

To fast means to put God first. There is a time to eat, drink, sleep and enjoy the blessings of a life. But there is also a time to turn our backs on it and seek God's face in times fasting and praying. When the devil tried to tempt Jesus to eat, he responded:

> "Man shall not live by bread alone, but by every word
> that proceeds from the mouth of the Lord."
> *(Matthew 4:4)*

Fasting is an attitude of the heart in which we interrupt our normal life to pray for a specific matter or cause. It symbolizes perseverance in prayer. And it is an effective way to remove obstacles and burdens. Fasting can also be a sign of sadness or mourning. In the Old Testament they often fasted as a sign of humiliation *(Leviticus 23:27)*. In its essence, it means tearing our hearts before God and confessing *(Joel 2:12-13)*.

The Lord also intended fasting to have an element of happiness and joy. Zechariah 8:19 says:

> "Thus says the Lord of hosts: 'The fast of the fourth month, the fast of the fifth, The fast of the seventh, And the fast of the tenth, shall be joy and gladness and cheerful feasts for the house of Judah. Therefore love truth and peace."

The Old Testament outlines the attitude we should have whilst fasting and praying. Isaiah 58:6-7 says:

> "Is this not the fast that I have chosen: To loose the bonds of wickedness, to undo the heavy burdens, to let the oppressed go free, and that you break every yoke? Is it not to share your bread with the hungry, and that you bring to your house the poor who are cast out; when you see the naked, that you cover him, and not hide yourself from your own flesh?"

THE PURPOSE OF FASTING

How does fasting impact our prayers? Fasting adds urgency to our prayer. When the nation of Israel was close to being destroyed, Esther declared a fast. Esther 4:16-17 says:

> "Go, gather all the Jews who are present in Shushan, and fast for me; neither eat nor drink for three days, night or day. My maids and I will fast likewise. And so I will go to the king, which is against the law; and if I perish, I perish!"

When we increase the urgency of our prayers we reap benefits.

First, fasting produces purity.

During fasting, physical appetites are denied in the battle between the flesh and the spirit. Fasting starves the flesh and feeds the spirit (*1 Corinthians. 9:27, Matthew 16:24*).

Second, fasting produces guidance.

Our spiritual senses are awakened during fasting. This awakening positions us to hear from God clearly. Acts 13:2 says:

> "While they were worshiping the Lord and fasting, the Holy Spirit said, "Set apart for me Barnabas and Saul for the work to which I have called them."

Third, fasting causes revival.

Fasting quickens our dry or dead spirit. It stirs a deep hunger for God (*Isaiah. 58:9, Daniel. 9:1-3, Jonah 3:5-10*).

Fourth, fasting releases power.

Power to live a victorious Christian life. After fasting for forty days, Luke 4:14 says:

> "Jesus retuned to Galilee in the power of the Spirit, and news about him spread through the whole countryside."

Matthew 17: 19-21 says:

> "Then the disciples came to Jesus privately and said, 'Why could we not cast it out?' So Jesus said to them, 'Because of your unbelief; for assuredly, I say to you, if

you have faith as a mustard seed, you will say to this mountain, "Move from here to there," and it will move; and nothing will be impossible for you. However, this kind does not go out except by prayer and fasting.'"

The pouring out of God's Spirit in Joel 2:28-30 is preceded by a call to fasting *(Joel 1:4, 2:12, 2:15).*

Fifth, fasting produces healing.

It is considered to be the oldest and most effective healing known to man. Throughout its long medical history, fasting has been regarded as one of most dependable curative and rejuvenate measures. Hippocrates, "the father of medicine." prescribed it. So did Paracelsus, and all the other great physicians of old. Paracelsus called fasting "the greatest remedy, the physician within."

THE PRACTICE OF FASTING

Jesus says in Matthew 6:17-18:

"But when you fast, put oil on your head and wash your face, so that it will not be obvious to men that you are fasting, but only to your Father, who is unseen; and your Father, who sees what is done in secret, will reward you."

Your fasting should be based on the conviction that God's Word enjoins this as part of normal Christian life. Do not set yourself too long a period of fasting to begin with.

During your fast, devote plenty of time to Bible reading.

Set specific objectives in your fasting; such as, personal sanctification, intercession, special burdens, divine intervention, blessing, and spiritual fullness for self or others, to stay divine wrath, and bring revival.

Avoid religious ostentation and boastfulness. Remember that fasting does not earn you merit with God. It is part of your duty as a committed Christian.

Check your motives anytime you fast *(Matthew. 6:16-18)*.

FASTING VARIES IN LENGTH

- **One night** - praying through the night. *(Daniel 6:18, 2 Corinthians. 6:4-5, 2 Corinthians. 11:27)*.

- **One day** - *(1 Samuel. 14:24, 2 Samuel. 3:35)*. For those fasting for the first time it is advisable that you begin the day with warm water with a little honey added.

- **Three days** - (Esther 4:15-16, Acts 9:9).

    Day I - mouth tastes ashy and sour.

    Day 2 - sharp pangs and weakness.

    Day 3 - relief from pain and feeling of light headedness. Energy is restored.

- **Seven days** - (1 Samuel 31:13, 2 Samuel 12:16-18).

- **Fourteen days** - (Acts 27:33-35).

- **Twenty-one days** - *(Daniel 10:2-3)*

- **Forty days** - *(Exodus 34:28, Deuteronomy 9:9, 1 Kings 19:8, Matthew 4:2)*

During fasting, expect hunger *(Matthew 4:2)*, weakness *(Psalm 109-24)*, and headaches and/or bad breath.

Finally, put yourself on a schedule. For maximum spiritual benefit, set aside ample time to be alone with the Lord. Listen for His leading. The more time you spend with Him, the more meaningful your fast will be.

Morning

- Begin your day in praise and worship.

- Read and meditate on God's Word, preferably on your knees.

- Invite the Holy Spirit to work in you to will and to do His good pleasure according to Philippians 2:13.

- Invite God to use you. Ask Him to show you how to influence your world, your family, your church, your community, your country, and beyond.

- Pray for His vision for your life and empowerment to do His will.

Noon

- Return to prayer and God's Word.

- Take a short prayer walk.

Spend time in intercessory prayer for your community's and nation's leaders, for the world's unreached millions, for your family or special needs.

Evening

- Get alone for an unhurried time of "seeking His face."

- If others are fasting with you, meet together for prayer.

- Avoid television or any other distraction that may dampen your spiritual focus.

- End Your fast gradually and expect results.

CHAPTER EIGHT

THE PASSIONS OF A PRAYING SAVIOUR

John chapter 17 is actually the "Lord's Prayer". We sometimes refer to the one He taught His disciples as the "Lord's Prayer". That's not really His prayer. That was the disciples' prayer. The disciples approached Him and asked Him to teach them how to pray. Then Jesus said, "When you pray, pray like this". That couldn't have been His prayer because Jesus would never ever pray "Forgive us our trespasses." Jesus never sinned. The point is that He modelled a prayer for the disciples.

The real prayer of Jesus is found in the Gospel of chapter John 17. It is the longest recorded prayer of our Lord Jesus Christ. Here we see the most intimate glimpse anywhere in scripture of the mind and the heart of the Lord as He led in prayer. I believe the mind and the heart of a person is revealed in their intimate prayers. If you want to know where somebody's agenda is, and where there priorities are, secretly go behind them and listen as they pray.

To know and understand the passions and the priorities of the Savior we need to study afresh John 17. Let me summarize them:

He Prayed that He Might be Glorified

John 17:1-5 says:

> "Jesus spoke these words, lifted up His eyes to heaven,
> and said: 'Father, the hour has come. Glorify Your Son,
> that Your Son also may glorify You, as You have given
> Him authority over all flesh, that He should give eternal
> life to as many as You have given Him. And this is eternal
> life, that they may know You, the only true God, and Je-
> sus Christ whom You have sent. I have glorified You on
> the earth. I have finished the work which You have given
> Me to do. And now, O Father, glorify Me together with
> Yourself, with the glory which I had with You before the
> world was'."

Our primary purpose in life is not to make money, although
money is good. Our primary purpose in life is not to get
married, although marriage is good. Our primary purpose is
not to be happy, although happiness is good. Our primary
purpose in life is to GLORIFY JESUS! That is why you are
here, that is why you breathe, that is why you live and have
your being. In Isaiah 43:6-7:

> "I will say to the north, 'Give them up!' And to the south,
> 'Do not keep them back!' Bring My sons from afar, And
> My daughters from the ends of the earth. Everyone who
> is called by My name, whom I have created for My glory;
> I have formed him, yes, I have made him."

God is gathering, redeeming, and calling His people for
Himself for the sole purpose of glorifying His name. How
do we glorify God?

The first way we glorify God is when we sing. We gather together first and foremost to worship Him. Our gathering is not to lift the pastor up, or any other person for that matter. Our gathering is to lift Him up! When Isaiah saw the angels before the throne he said, "each one had six wings: with two he covered his face, with two he covered his feet, and with two he flew". Worship is not about us. We need to, symbolically, cover our faces.. Psalm 50:23, *"Whoever offers praise glorifies Me"*. When God's people pray, they glorify Jesus, and we need to be excited to glorify Him. For this is why we are created.

The second way we glorify Jesus is when we shine. Matthew 5:14-16:

> "You are the light of the world. A city that is set on a hill cannot be hidden. Nor do they light a lamp and put it under a basket, but on a lampstand, and it gives light to all who are in the house. Let your light so shine before men, that they may see your good works and glorify your Father in heaven."

This means we are to be careful how we live. Our lives can bring Him glory or bring Him shame.

The third way we glorify Jesus is when we serve Him. God has given every one of us gifts and talents. We glorify Him when we use them. 1 Peter 4:10-11:

> "As each one has received a gift, minister it to one another, as good stewards of the manifold grace of God. If anyone speaks, let him speak as the oracles of God. If anyone

ministers, let him do it as with the ability which God supplies, that in all things God may be glorified through Jesus Christ, to whom belong the glory and the dominion forever and ever. Amen."

The final way we glorify God is when we suffer. Suffering is the price we pay to follow Jesus. This includes choosing to stay holy. The Bible says "Yes, and all who desire to live godly in Christ Jesus will suffer persecution." *(2 Timothy 3:12)*

Mathew 5:10 says:

"Blessed are those who are persecuted for righteousness' sake, for theirs is the kingdom of heaven."

He Prayed that We Might be Sanctified

John 17:14, *"I have given them your Word… "*. Now He turns His attention from His glory to the disciples. Being a child of God and living in the world is a difficult task. Jesus did not pray to keep us out of the world but for us to be sanctified in the world. The word "sanctify" means to set apart; to set aside; to separate; or to be made holy. Let me explain. In the Old Testament when any object is taken from among the people and placed in the temple it becomes sanctified. Why? It has been set aside for the sole purpose of being in the temple. There is no intrinsic holiness in the object. But it has been made holy because it is set aside.

So this is what Jesus is saying, "They are in the world. But separate them from the world." Sanctification is a process.

First, God sanctifies us through the Scriptures.

Jesus said, *"Sanctify them by Your truth. Your Word is truth" (John 17:17)*. The way God helps us to be set apart is that He has given us His Word. It points to the truth. It exposes the lies of world. It tells us that God is good and has a wonderful plan for us. It tells us that sin will never satisfy us. He tells us that joy comes through our Lord and Savior Jesus Christ.

Second, we are sanctified through the Spirit.

He is at work in us. He convicts us when we sin; He warns us when we are entering into temptation; and He encourages us when we feel like giving up.

Third, we are sanctified by the Saints.

God places people in our lives to help us stay holy. Don't push them away. I have intentionally surrounded myself with people who are helping me grow. They have my permission to warn me when they sense I am going wayward. The Bible says:

> "As iron sharpens iron, so a man sharpens the countenance of his friend." *(Proverbs 27:17)*

He Prayed that We Might Be United

John 17:20-21:

> "I do not pray for these alone, but also for those who will believe in Me through their word; that they all may be

one, as You, Father, are in Me, and I in You; that they also may be one in Us, that the world may believe that You sent Me."

This is the heart of God. That we may be one. And it is not a sentimental or superficial oneness. He said "Let them be one, just as we are". It is the same kind of oneness between Jesus and the Father. In Ephesians 4:3-6 Paul says we must do everything possible to keep this unity:

"endeavoring to keep the unity of the Spirit in the bond of peace. There is one body and one Spirit, just as you were called in one hope of your calling; one Lord, one faith, one baptism; one God and Father of all, who is above all, and through all, and in you all."

The reason why unity is so difficult to keep is that we are all so different. Our differences tend to divide us. But actually God intended our differences to bring us together. For example, that's why God made a man and woman so different. Galatians 3:27-28:

"For as many of you as were baptized into Christ have put on Christ. There is neither Jew nor Greek, there is neither slave nor free, there is neither male nor female; for you are all one in Christ Jesus."

God created the Jews, Greeks, Caribbean, Caucasian, African and Asian. He didn't make us different to hate each other but to love each other. Our differences are meant to be celebrated. That is why He wants His church to be a church of all nations. We are meant to come together. We are not meant to be divided. We are not meant to go to our own little white, black or brown church. The color of our skin should not separate us. There is no black or white church in heaven. Revelation 7:9-10 says:

> "After these things I looked, and behold, a great multitude which no one could number, of all nations, tribes, peoples, and tongues, standing before the throne and before the Lamb, clothed with white robes, with palm branches in their hands, and crying out with a loud voice, saying, Salvation belongs to our God who sits on the throne, and to the Lamb."

Psalm133:1-3:

> "Behold, how good and how pleasant it is for brethren to dwell together in unity! It is like the precious oil upon the head, running down on the beard, the beard of Aaron, running down on the edge of his garments. It is like the dew of Hermon, descending upon the mountains of Zion; For there the LORD commanded the blessing—life forevermore."

Unity is where He commands blessing. It is where He commands His refreshment. Unity is where He commands His anointing. That is why it is so important. There is power in oneness.

He Prayed that the World Might Be Evangelized

Finally, Jesus turned His attention to the lost. John 17:18-20:

"As You sent Me into the world, I also have sent them into the world. And for their sakes I sanctify Myself, that they also may be sanctified by the truth. "I do not pray for these alone, but also for those who will believe in Me through their word."

There is a lost world out there. In Luke 15, Jesus talked about the parable of the lost sheep; the parable of the lost silver; and the parable of the lost son. It doesn't matter how they look; where they live; or what they drive. They are lost!

The sad thing is that judgment is soon coming. God does not want anyone to perish. 1 Peter 3 says: *"He doesn't wish that any should be destroyed".* That's why He keeps on delaying! Heaven is real and beautiful. But hell is real and awful. Revelation 20 makes it clear that hell was not created for us but for the devil and his angels. That is why we must go to all nations. Paul says in 2 Corinthians 5:10-11:

"For we must all appear before the judgment seat of Christ, that each one may receive the things done in the body, according to what he has done, whether good or bad. Knowing, therefore, the terror of the Lord, we persuade men; but we are well known to God, and I also trust are well known in your consciences."

We have a divine obligation to tell the whole world about the Good News. How do we do that?

First by our love. The story of the Good Samaritan tells us how to express sacrificial love to a dying world (*Luke 10:25-37).*

Second we share the Gospel by our life. We might be the only Jesus people will meet. So let it count.

Finally we share the Gospel by our lips. Tell them Jesus loves them. Tell them He has a wonderful plan for their life.

May the prayer of our Savior Jesus Christ

be fulfilled in our lives.